Motivator

-Composition and Dialogue-

会話と表現のクラスワーク

高橋哲郎

Nan'un-do

Download Audio

音声ファイル
無料 DL
のご案内

このテキストの音声を無料で視聴（ストリーミング）・ダウンロードできます。自習用音声としてご活用ください。
以下のサイトにアクセスしてテキスト番号で検索してください。

https://nanun-do.com　テキスト番号［**512041**］

※ 無線 LAN（WiFi）に接続してのご利用を推奨いたします。

※ 音声ダウンロードは Zip ファイルでの提供になります。
お使いの機器によっては別途ソフトウェア（アプリケーション）の導入が必要となります。

Motivator
-Composition and Dialogue-

はしがき

（本書の特色・方針）

意欲的に学習できるかどうかは、まずは成果への期待が持続できるかにかかっています（期待構造／promising system）。

特に外国語の場合、ふだん使っている母国語の熟達と絶えず比較されてしまうことから、目に見える成果がいち早く欲しくなり、それだけに改善が見られないと意欲も失われてしまうのが実情でしょう。

第二に、言葉は日常的な必然があってこそ身につくもので、日本における外国語教育にはその視点が十分備わっていないと感じています。

情報を収集せざるを得ない場面、意見を交換したくなる設定、そういった工夫が向学心を内側から押し上げてくれます。

最後に見直したいのが想像力を使った発信（imagine-out）による主体性の啓発です。

私自身大学で教鞭をとらせて頂くようになってからも、舞台や放送の脚本を執筆し、作家や演技のワークショップなどを開催してきましたが、若い表現者や製作者に劣らず、学生たちにも「自ら伝えたい」という欲動が潜在しています。シミュレーション学習（ロールプレイ）に有効な会話や関係性の想像は、誰もが日頃から無意識に行なっている行為でもあり、学生たちが主体的に学ぶための鍵を握っています。

本書は、シンプルな例文や基本的な練習を通し、短いスパンで着実な成果が感じられるよう構成されています。

身近な写真を契機に「伝えたい／問いたい」という気持ちを発動させ、必然に応じて文法を復習し、完成された会話を参考にしながらペアワークなどで独自のやり取りを作り上げ、語彙や語法をマスターしていく。そんな流れを念頭に置いています。

写真に端を発する想像会話の作成は、実際の学生生活や、個々に関心のある雑誌記事に及んでもいいでしょう。指示一つで、学習者がそれぞれ教材を持ち寄り、結果的に数冊のテキストに相当する展開性も秘めていると考えます。

この教科書を使用した授業から、より実践的で広がりのある外国語学習へと、成果への期待を繰り上げて行ってもらえれば幸いです。

本書の作成にあたり、南雲堂の加藤敦様には大変お世話になりました。あらためて御礼申し上げます。

著者

使い方
（構成）

学習する文法事項と、テーマを含む会話が生まれる場面（設定）がユニットのタイトルになっています。解答は学習者同士でチェックし合うほか、別紙に記入、ないし教科書ごと教員に提出することも可能です。英作文についても、原則的には資料の模範解答（複数）を紹介、添削はグループごとに精査され提出されたものに対して行なうと良いでしょう。

●各ユニットの 1 ページ目（Picture）
学生にとって理解しやすい（作りやすい）文章を想起させる写真を掲載してあります。写真下の例文に従い、描写文を作ってください。その際、写真の目の付け所や簡単なストーリー（3 ページ目の会話がその例）を話し合うなどすると作成が捗るでしょう。

● 2 ページ目（Grammar）
1 ページ目の英作文に必要な文法がまとめられています。左右のページを往復しながら学習することもできます。簡素な説明と最小限の例文（練習問題）から成っており、使いやすく理解もしやすいですが、問題を適宜追加して頂いても構いません。

● 3 ページ目（Dialogue）
具体的な設定と人物から成る英語会話が掲載されています。1 ページ目の写真の描写文とそれを聞き出す質問文とのセットをまず作り、人間関係や会話の目的を明らかにしてから、語句や流れの理解に進んでください。またキーワードやキーセンテンスを意識しながら音読することで、やり取りの呼吸なども感得できます。

● 4 ページ目（Create a dialogue）
最終段階として、ペアになりオリジナルの会話を創作してもらいます。短い英文をいくつか作り組み合わせることをゴールとし、達成感を多く味わうことを優先させます。ただ出来上がった会話文については、何回か読み合わせ、発音・語順・切り方・強弱・目線の 5 項目について客観的に評価し合うことをお薦めします。複数の学生に同時に、また主体的に参加してもらえる練習の記録であり、成績の作成に直結させられるページです。

Contents

Unit 1

動詞と語順 …………………… 印象を話す

●以下の写真の描写文の空所に、下の語群から適語を選んで（必要なら形を変えて）補充しましょう。
動詞を重視

写真Ⓐ

① They ______ students.

② One of the boys is ______ a white T-shirt.

③ They ______ down the steps.

④ They ______ to each other.

⑤ The leaves on the trees ______ green.

写真Ⓑ

① Three cups ______ on the table.

② The cups ______ different colors.

③ One girl ______ a photo of them.

④ They ______ themselves on a smart phone.

⑤ They don't ______, but they smile.

語群

状態：am, are, is

動作：go, take, talk, watch, wear, have

Grammar（動詞の種類）

英文では S（主語 subject）のあとに、状態（be 動詞）や動作（一般動詞）を表す語句 V（動詞 verb）が来ます。

●状態（be 動詞）

I am from Kyoto.

He is a baseball player.

They are happy to be here.

動作無しで成立する英文における動詞を「be 動詞」といい、**単数か複数により am/is/are を使い分けます。**

●動作（一般動詞）

I run around the park every morning.

She watches TV after studying.

Students think of their future.

上記の文は、主語の身体の一部もしくは全部が動いています（have, know など例外もあります）。

このように「動作」を表す動詞を「一般動詞」といい、**S が単数のときは末尾に -s/-es をつけます。**

●過去形

過去の状態・動作を表す場合、be 動詞は was/were、一般動詞は末尾に d/ed/ied をつけて用います（不規則に変化するものもあります）。（　）内の動詞を適切な形に直し、空所を補充しましょう。

① He ______ a football player before.（be）

② They ______ surprised to hear the news yesterday.（be）

③ She ______ a movie last night.（watch）

④ I ______ a letter and posted it last week.（write）

●否定

be 動詞は後ろに not、一般動詞は前に don't/doesn't/didn't を入れます。補充しましょう。

① I ______ ______ from Tokyo.

② My sister ______ eat breakfast.

③ The children ______ know the end of the story.

▶ be 動詞の英文を自由に作ってみましょう。

Dialogue

●設定

関係：新入生同士

目的：学校の印象を話し合う

●会話例（空所に適文を選んで記号を入れなさい）02

On campus, on the first day of the term:

YOU: I walked around the campus yesterday.

YOUR FRIEND: Me too. (1)

YOU: It has many buildings, doesn't it?

YOUR FRIEND: Yes.

YOU: The campus is large. I need to use a map for now.

YOUR FRIEND: I almost got lost, even with a map. (2)
I found the cafeteria yesterday, though.

YOU: Really? I didn't find it.

YOUR FRIEND: I didn't go inside. (3)

YOU: I see. The buildings here are clean.

YOUR FRIEND: Students love the new, modern buildings.

YOU: My high school was rather old and not very clean.

YOUR FRIEND: Mine was also old and there was no cafeteria.

YOU: I'm dreaming of going there someday.

YOUR FRIEND: Dream? Someday? You are a student here.

YOU: This bicycle parking lot feels familiar.

YOUR FRIEND: (4)

YOU: It's old and dirty! Maybe that's why we feel comfortable and can speak so freely.

YOUR FRIEND: You're right.

ア It was too clean for me.
イ I want to know more about my university.
ウ Yes, it's an old place.
エ We don't have a sense of direction.

Ⓐキーワードやキーセンテンスを指摘しましょう。

Ⓑ補充された会話を聴いた上で、上記の会話例をペアで音読してみましょう。

Create a dialogue

今までの作業を踏まえ、ペアになってオリジナルの会話を作成しましょう（提出は別紙を使用してもいい）。

Ⓐこの Unit の最初のページを参考に「学校の印象を描写する」英文を 3 つ作成しましょう。

① ______________________________.

② ______________________________.

③ ______________________________.

Ⓑ上記の英文を組み合わせた会話原稿を作成し音読してみましょう。

Ⓒ第三者に聞いてもらい、感想を自己評価の参考にしましょう（各項 2 点満点、他の項目を加えてもいい）。

①発音、アクセント　（　　　　点）

②語順、文法　（　　　　点）

③切り方　（　　　　点）

④強弱　（　　　　点）

⑤目線　（　　　　点）　（合計　　　　/10 点）

Ⓓ印象を話す際に使われる語句をリストアップしましょう（オリジナル作成時に用いた語句も追加）。

① be far from having ～ : ～なんてありそうにない

②

③

④

⑤

Unit 2

補語と目的語 …………………… スケジュールを知る

●動詞の補充

Ⓐ写真の人物の一日について想像し、下の語群から適切なものを選んで空所を補いましょう。

① I ________ a high school student.

② I ________ far from my school, so I get up at 6:00 and leave without eating enough breakfast.

③ I ________ a bus to the nearest station, and ________ a train from there.

④ The first class ________ at 8:40.

⑤ I ________ four classes in the morning.

⑥ I ________ sleepy in the morning.

⑦ My lunch break ________ from 12:40 to 13:30.

⑧ I ________ lacrosse after school as a club activity.

⑨ I ________ home at 8:00 p.m., and sometimes have a light meal before I leave.

⑩ I ________ to study at 9:00 p.m.

⑪ At around 10:00 p.m., I ________ for tomorrow's classes, and take a bath.

⑫ I usually ________ to music or browse the internet before going to bed at 11:00 p.m.

語群

return, begin, am, live, have, take, prepare, listen, is, begins, are, play

Grammar（補語と目的語）

●英語の文章は SV のあと、**補語 C（S の補足）**や**目的語 O（V の目的）**が続く場合があります。

She is relaxing.

People study English.

●**副詞句**が、時や場など「詳しい情報」を追加します。

She is relaxing with her friends.

People study English at school.

● SV それぞれに形容詞や副詞などの、修飾語句がついて、前後から説明を追加します。

Usually, Japanese people study English in high school.

●補語と目的語

Ⓐ SV 後の補語または目的語を「自由に」補充して、意味の通る文にしましょう。

① She is ______________________________.

② She has ______________________________.

③ They are ______________________________.

④ My brother eats ______________________________.

Ⓑそれぞれ選んで下の欄に英文を作りましょう。

主語群 My father, The runner, His classmates, The musician, The artists, The manager, Children

動詞群（状態） is, are

補語群 sad, careful, careless, cheerful, curious, a driver, a salesperson, Korean, American

動詞群（動作） learns, wears, gets, paints, plays, opens, hires

目的語群 a jersey, the award, staff, dodgeball, history, a picture, the window

副詞群（時） in the morning, this time, usually, tonight, today, at last, this afternoon

副詞群（場） in the hall, in my house, here, on the ground, in the studio, around the park, at school

Dialogue

●設定
関係：大学の友人同士
目的：互いのスケジュールを知る

●会話例（空所に適文を選んで記号を入れなさい） 03

At the student lounge, you check your class schedule with your friend:

YOU: I want to take an art class. It's a general requirement.

YOUR FRIEND: I heard about it. The teacher is a famous movie director.

YOU: Yes, but there's a problem. I'm too busy.

YOUR FRIEND: Too busy?

YOU: (1)

YOUR FRIEND: You don't have enough leisure time.

YOU: I get up at 5:30 every day for my first class.
It takes more than two hours to get here.

YOUR FRIEND: (2)

YOU: I want to live alone near here.

YOUR FRIEND: My apartment is just three blocks away.

YOU: (3)

YOUR FRIEND: I walk here every day.

YOU: And you don't have any early classes.

YOUR FRIEND: I don't like to get up early, but I'm late for my 9 a.m. class today.

YOU: Late for your 9 o'clock class?

YOUR FRIEND: Maybe, (4)

YOU: But you live near the university, don't you?

YOUR FRIEND: I'm late because I live so close! I always sleep late.

ア You live far away from the university.
イ I take it too easy to arrive on time.
ウ I envy you.
エ I take four classes every day.

Ⓐキーワードやキーセンテンスを指摘しましょう。
Ⓑ補充された会話を聴いた上で、上記の会話例をペアで音読してみましょう。

Create a dialogue

今までの作業を踏まえ、ペアになってオリジナルの会話を作成しましょう（提出は別紙を使用してもいい）。

Ⓐこの Unit の最初のページを参考に「スケジュールについて表す」英文を 3 つ作成しましょう。

① .

② .

③ .

④ .

⑤ .

Ⓑ上記の英文を使って 6 行ほどの会話原稿を作成し音読してみましょう。

Ⓒ第三者に聞いてもらい、感想を自己評価の参考にしましょう（各項 2 点満点、他の項目を加えてもいい）。

①発音、アクセント　（　　　点）

②語順、文法　（　　　点）

③切り方　（　　　点）

④強弱　（　　　点）

⑤目線　（　　　点）　（合計　　　/10 点）

Ⓓスケジュールについて話すときに使われる語句をリストアップしましょう（オリジナル作成時に用いた語句も追加）。

① it takes more than ～ : ～以上時間が掛かる

②

③

④

⑤

Unit 3

疑問文の作り方……………………問題を述べる

●写真の人物の立場で想像し、例を参考に英語で書きなさい。

Ⓐ自己

① I am from Hokkaido.

② I run around the park every morning.

③ I am interested in fitness training.

④ ______________________________.

⑤ ______________________________.

Ⓑ通学

⑥ My home is far away from the university.

⑦ My commute here is very long.

⑧ I take two trains to get here.

⑨ ______________________________.

⑩ ______________________________.

Ⓒ生活

⑪ I'm sleepy in the morning.

⑫ I have a part-time job five days a week.

⑬ I don't have enough time to study.

⑭ ______________________________.

⑮ ______________________________.

Grammar（疑問文の作り方）

● be 動詞と一般動詞とでは疑問文の作り方が違うので注意しましょう。

He is a student. → Is he a student?

They are happy. → Are they happy?

●一般動詞の疑問文は、S が単数の場合 Does で始め、S が複数の場合は Do で始めます。

She laughs with her friends. → Does she laugh with her friends?

They write their study schedule. → Do they write their study schedule?

●質問 / 応答（be/ 一般）補充しましょう。

Ⓐ A teacher and student are in the classroom：be 動詞（状態）の文は be 動詞を先頭に

① Student: I'm from Aomori Prefecture.

Teacher: ＿＿＿＿＿ you accustomed to cold weather?

Student: Yes, ＿＿＿＿＿＿＿. / No, ＿＿＿＿＿＿＿.

② Student: My bag is very heavy.

Teacher: ＿＿＿＿＿ it filled with books?

Student: Yes, ＿＿＿＿＿＿＿. / No, ＿＿＿＿＿＿＿.

③ Student: My classmates are very sleepy this morning.

Teacher: ＿＿＿＿＿ they busy with their part-time jobs?

Student: Yes, ＿＿＿＿＿＿＿. / No, ＿＿＿＿＿＿＿.

Ⓑ Another member and you are in the club's room：一般動詞（動作）の文は do, does, did を前に

① You: I don't agree with the rules of our club.

Another member: ＿＿＿＿＿ you have an opinion about that?

You: Yes, ＿＿＿＿＿＿＿. / No, ＿＿＿＿＿＿＿.

② You: I want to join the club's summer program.

Another member: ＿＿＿＿＿ your parents allow you to go?

You: I ＿＿＿＿＿ them to let me go yesterday.　説得する：persuade

Dialogue

●描写と質問　前ページの英文を踏まえ、描写と質問の英文セットを作成。

I am interested in fitness training my body. − Are you interested in fitness training?

It takes a long time to get here. − Does it take a long time to get here?

My study time is rather short. − Is your study time rather short?

●設定

関係：学生と教員

目的：問題について話し合う

●会話例（空所に適文を選んで記号を入れなさい）04

On the university campus, a student and his English teacher meet:

STUDENT: Ms. Brown, uh... thank you for today's class.

TEACHER: You're welcome, Was it useful for you?

STUDENT: Frankly, I'm afraid I was a little sleepy.

TEACHER: Why are you sleepy? (　　1　　)

STUDENT: I live far away from the university.

TEACHER: Do you have a long commute?

STUDENT: Yes.　Second, (　　2　　)

TEACHER: Too bad.　Do you have enough time to study?

STUDENT: Yes.　I also run around the park every morning.

TEACHER: (　　3　　) Never forget it.

STUDENT: Sorry.　Basically, I'm poor at learning foreign languages.

TEACHER: Don't say that.　You run every morning, don't you?

STUDENT: Yes, I do.

TEACHER: Are you interested in fitness training?

STUDENT: Yes, I wanted to join a club, but I didn't.

TEACHER: You work part-time and run every day.　You're diligent and successful!

STUDENT: Am I diligent?

TEACHER: (　　4　　)

STUDENT: Studying is a little different from running.

㋐ I have a part-time job five days a week.

㋑ Don't give up on learning!

㋒ Don't you have enough time to sleep?

㋓ You're a student.

Ⓐキーワードやキーセンテンスを指摘しましょう。

Ⓑ補充された会話を聴いた上で、上記の会話例をペアで音読してみましょう。

Create a dialogue

今までの作業を踏まえ、ペアになってオリジナルの会話を作成しましょう（提出は別紙を使用してもいい）。

ⒶこのUnitの最初のページを参考に「スケジュールについて表す」英文を3つ作成しましょう。

① .

② .

③ .

ⒷこのUnitの2ページ目を参考に「問題を聴く」英文を3つ作成しましょう。

① .

② .

③ .

Ⓒ上記の英文を使って6行ほどの会話原稿を作成し音読してみましょう。

Ⓓ第三者に聞いてもらい、感想を自己評価の参考にしましょう（各項2点満点、他の項目を加えてもいい）。

①発音、アクセント　（　　　点）

②語順、文法　（　　　点）

③切り方　（　　　点）

④強弱　（　　　点）

⑤目線　（　　　点）　（合計　　　/10点）

Ⓔ問題を話し合うときに使われる語句をリストアップしましょう（オリジナル作成時に用いた語句も追加）。

① be poor at 〜 ing：〜するのが苦手

②

③

④

⑤

Unit 4

疑問文に替える……状況を知り合う

●写真の人物の立場で想像し、例を参考に英語で書きなさい。

Ⓐ自己

① I'm from Okinawa.

② I live near the university.

③ I like dancing.

④ ____.

⑤ ____.

Ⓑ授業

⑥ English is difficult for me.

⑦ I'll preview the lesson.

⑧ I'm good at listening.

⑨ ____.

⑩ ____.

Ⓒサークル

⑪ This university has some dance clubs.

⑫ I belonged to a cheerleading club.

⑬ I found a good dance club.

⑭ ____.

⑮ ____.

Grammar（疑問文に替える）

●下線部を疑問文に直しなさい（I は you に変えて）。

Ⓐ Mana introduces herself.

My name is Mana. I'm a third-year university student. I attended the job fair last week. I'm a little nervous because job-hunting is difficult. ①I was shy as a child, but my personality changed after being the equipment manager of the baseball club. Now ②I'm aggressive about setting goals and overcoming weaknesses. I'm also learning to consider other people's feelings. We all want to act together to try to understand each other. It's one of our essential feelings. So, ③I'm also interested in volunteering. I want to help troubled people.

To understand each other, ④I think it is also important to obtain information. So, I'd like to get a media-related job. I've had part-time jobs at some media companies and took extra mass communication classes. But ⑤I regret not having studied abroad. Though I've taken TOEIC test several times, I can't hear nor understand English well. I'll take an English conversation class for now. I want to improve my command of English as soon as possible.

Ⓑ Kenta introduces himself.

I'm Kenta. I'm a member of the animation club. I like not only watching animation but also making animated films. Last year, when I was a freshman, ①I was in a club. We watched animation made by Hayao Miyazaki and Makoto Shinkai. However, I want to create original animation and tell my story.

But there's just one problem, I don't have anything dramatic in my real life to inspire me! I don't have enough inspiration to create drama from my daily life. What is drama? One of my friends told me, ②"Drama contains either success or a breakdown." I think both are the result of one's effort to realize a dream. I should have a dream first. But ③it's difficult for me to determine my dream. To be sure, ④I hope to be an animator, but I don't know how to do it. Anyway I'll watch many animated films and read many comics and books.

⑤My university offers some literature classes. We'll study various ways to craft a story. Maybe I'll learn how to create drama. The process of discovering a topic might create drama.

Ⓒそれぞれの目的に合った疑問文を作りましょう。

①留学を計画しているかを訊く。

②先月何か映画を観たかを訊く。

③彼が高校時代バスケットボールの選手だったかを訊く。

④彼女がクラシック音楽を聴くことが好きかを訊く。

⑤自分の母親が写真を撮ることに興味を持っているかを訊く。

Dialogue

●描写と質問　前ページの英文を踏まえ、描写と質問の英文セットを作成。

I like dancing. − Do you like dancing?

I preview the lessons. − Do you preview the lessons?

I found a good dance club. − Did you find a good dance club?

●設定

関係：同じクラスの学生

目的：状況を知り合う

●会話例（空所に適文を選んで記号を入れなさい）05

In the classroom, following the afternoon class:

YOU: Our first class is over.

SAKURA: English is difficult for me.

YOU: Me, too. Do you preview the lessons?

SAKURA: Yes, I preview the lessons.

YOU: Do you have enough free time? Do you belong to any clubs?

SAKURA: (　　1　　)

YOU: Do you like dancing?

SAKURA: Yes, I like dancing.

YOU: Does this university have a dance club?

SAKURA: Yes. (　　2　　)

YOU: I didn't know that. Did you find a good dance club?

SAKURA: Yes, I found a good dance club yesterday.

YOU: Good. I want to join a club, but I still need time to preview my English lessons.

SAKURA: (　　3　　)

YOU: Do you mean the English Speaking Society?

SAKURA: Yes. (　　4　　)

YOU: I want to play a sport or dance, like you.

ア This university is also famous for ESS.
イ No, I'm looking for a dance club.
ウ This university is famous for its dance clubs.
エ Let's study English and preview the lessons.

Ⓐキーワードやキーセンテンスに下線を指摘しましょう。

Ⓑ補充された会話を聴いた上で、上記の会話例をペアで音読してみましょう。

Create a dialogue

今までの作業を踏まえ、ペアになってオリジナルの会話を作成しましょう（提出は別紙を使用してもいい）。

Ⓐこの Unit の最初のページを参考に「状況やパーソナリティを表す」英文を 3 つ作成しましょう。

① ______________________________.

② ______________________________.

③ ______________________________.

Ⓑこの Unit の 2 ページ目を参考に「状況やパーソナリティを聴く」英文を 3 つ作成しましょう。

① ______________________________.

② ______________________________.

③ ______________________________.

Ⓒ上記の英文を使って 6 行ほどの会話原稿を作成し音読してみましょう。

Ⓓ第三者に聞いてもらい、感想を自己評価の参考にしましょう（各項 2 点満点、他の項目を加えてもいい）。

①発音、アクセント（　　点）

②語順、文法（　　点）

③切り方（　　点）

④強弱（　　点）

⑤目線（　　点）（合計　　/10 点）

Ⓔ状況を知り合うときに使われる語句をリストアップしましょう（オリジナル作成時に用いた語句も追加）。

① be famous for ～：～で有名である

②

③

④

⑤

Unit 5

助動詞 アドバイスをもらう

●写真の人物の立場で想像し、例を参考に英語で書きなさい。

Ⓐ自己

① I am a freshman.

② I can do it by myself.

③ This university may suit me.

④ ____.

⑤ ____.

Ⓑ趣味

⑥ My hobby is cycling.

⑦ We are going to travel by bicycle.

⑧ I will check my bicycle.

⑨ ____.

⑩ ____.

Ⓒ目標

⑪ A study schedule is necessary.

⑫ I have to acquire some qualifications.

⑬ In particular, I must study foreign languages.

⑭ ____.

⑮ ____.

Grammar（助動詞）

●助動詞の種類

助動詞は、動詞の前に入って意味合いを加えます。

未来の will、可能の can に加え、may（してもよい / かもしれない）、may が強まった must（しないといけない / にちがいない）、must 同様に義務を表す should, ought to, have(has) to も使えるようにしましょう。

Ⓐ（　　）内の日本語を参考に、空所に適切な英語を入れなさい。

① He ＿＿＿＿＿＿ come here at once.（来るつもりだ）

② They ＿＿＿＿＿＿ ＿＿＿＿＿＿ ＿＿＿＿＿＿ come tonight.（来ることになっている）

③ He ＿＿＿＿＿＿ play all these instruments.（弾くことができる）

= He is able to play all these instruments.

④ She ＿＿＿＿＿＿ speak Chinese back then.（話すことができた）

≠ She was not able to speak Chinese in those days.（継続的な可能は could）

⑤ They ＿＿＿＿＿＿ ＿＿＿＿＿＿ be late for the meeting.（はずがない）

⑥ He ＿＿＿＿＿＿ like joking.（好きかもしれない）

⑦ He ＿＿＿＿＿＿ like joking.（に違いない）

⑧ You ＿＿＿＿＿＿ ＿＿＿＿＿＿ enter this room.（入ってはいけない）

⑨ We ＿＿＿＿＿＿ invite him to our party.（招待するべき）

⑩ We don't ＿＿＿＿＿＿ ＿＿＿＿＿＿ prepare for the party.（準備しなくてもいい）

Ⓑ①②を疑問文に、⑥⑦を否定文に変えなさい。

① ＿＿＿＿＿＿＿＿＿＿＿＿＿＿＿＿＿＿＿＿ ?

② ＿＿＿＿＿＿＿＿＿＿＿＿＿＿＿＿＿＿＿＿ ?

⑥ ＿＿＿＿＿＿＿＿＿＿＿＿＿＿＿＿＿＿＿＿ .

⑦ ＿＿＿＿＿＿＿＿＿＿＿＿＿＿＿＿＿＿＿＿ .

Dialogue

●描写と質問　前ページの英文を踏まえ、描写と質問の英文セットを作成。

①I can do it by myself. – Can you do it by yourself?

②I will check my bicycle. – Will you check your bicycle?

③A study schedule is necessary. – Is a study schedule necessary?

●設定

関係：同じクラスの学生

目的：アドバイスをもらう

●会話例（空所に適文を選んで記号を入れなさい） 06

At the café, after school:

YOU: Can you do it by yourself?

DAIKI: Can you?

YOU: The teacher says "you must have a goal and make an effort toward realizing it."

DAIKI: You must have a hobby, and you should make time to enjoy it.

YOU: (　　1　　)

DAIKI: My hobby is cycling. We're going to travel by bicycle on our next holiday.

YOU: You must prepare many things for your holiday. Will you check your bicycle?

DAIKI: Yes, It's one of the most important things.

YOU: You have a goal and you can do better.

DAIKI: (　　2　　)

YOU: Is a study schedule necessary for studying?

DAIKI: Of course, it is. I have to take some tests.

YOU: That sounds difficult.

DAIKI: (　　3　　)

YOU: Do you mean TOEIC or TOEFL?

DAIKI: We have to learn about various communication tools.

YOU: (　　4　　)

DAIKI: You certainly will. You can practice English with me, to prepare for the test.

㋐ We have to have a schedule to meet our goals.

㋑ Will I able to master them?

㋒ In particular, I must study a foreign language.

㋓ Do you have any hobbies?

Ⓐキーワードやキーセンテンスを指摘しましょう。

Ⓑ補充された会話を聴いた上で、上記の会話例をペアで音読してみましょう。

Create a dialogue

今までの作業を踏まえ、ペアになってオリジナルの会話を作成しましょう（提出は別紙を使用してもいい）。

Ⓐこの Unit の最初のページを参考に「相手の状況にアドバイスをする」英文を 3 つ作成しましょう。

① ______________________.

② ______________________.

③ ______________________.

Ⓑこの Unit の 2 ページ目を参考に「相手からアドバイスをもらう」英文を 3 つ作成しましょう。

① ______________________.

② ______________________.

③ ______________________.

Ⓒ上記の英文を使って 6 行ほどの会話原稿を作成し音読してみましょう。

Ⓓ第三者に聞いてもらい、感想を自己評価の参考にしましょう（各項 2 点満点、他の項目を加えてもいい）。

①発音、アクセント　（　　　　点）

②語順、文法　（　　　　点）

③切り方　（　　　　点）

④強弱　（　　　　点）

⑤目線　（　　　　点）　（合計　　　　/10 点）

Ⓔアドバイスを交わすときに使われる語句をリストアップしましょう（オリジナル作成時に用いた語句も追加）。

① it takes time to ～：～するのに時間がかかる

②

③

④

⑤

疑問詞の文の作り方……………………仕事について

●写真の人物の立場で想像し、例を参考に英語で書きなさい。

Ⓐ自己

① I bought a computer yesterday.

② I moved to this town a month ago.

③ I'm going to meet my brother.

④ ____________________.

⑤ ____________________.

Ⓑ学校

⑥ My school is on a mountainside.

⑦ I borrowed some books from the library.

⑧ We'll have a midterm exam this week.

⑨ ____________________.

⑩ ____________________.

Ⓒアルバイト

⑪ I work at a convenience store.

⑫ The manager teaches employees how to do their jobs.

⑬ Many customers come to the store.

⑭ ____________________.

⑮ ____________________.

Grammar（疑問詞の文の作り方）

●疑問詞（what, who, when, where, why, how…）＋ be 動詞または Do/Does で始まる疑問文

Ⓐ She knows ❶the facts ❷exactly.

→❶を問う　What does she know exactly?
→❷を問う　How does she know the facts?

Ⓑ He bought ❶a computer ❷at the shop ❸yesterday.

→❶を問う　What did he buy at the shop yesterday?
→❷を問う　Where did he buy a computer yesterday?
→❸を問う　When did he buy a computer at the shop?

＊ S を問う場合は、疑問詞を S として以下のように作成。
→ Who knows the facts exactly?
→ Who bought a computer at the shop yesterday?

●質問／応答

Ⓐ Your brother/sister and you are at their home :

① You: I'm tired just from going to school.
Your sister: Where ________ your school?
You: It ________ on a mountainside.

② You: Economics is too difficult for me. I ________ at my wit's end!
Your brother: Why ________ you studying so hard?
You: We have an exam on Friday.

Ⓑ The manager and you are at the convenience store :

① Manager: You should master these tasks.
You: I'm worried about how I can master them. What kind of tasks ________ I master?
Manager: First, put the products on the shelves.

② Manager: We are very busy every weekend. When ________ you come next Saturday?
You: I can come early in the morning because I will be free all day.
Manager: Good. Will you ________ at 7 o'clock?

Dialogue

●描写と質問 前ページの英文を踏まえ、描写と質問の英文セットを作成。

I moved to this town a month ago. – When did you move to this town?

We will have a midterm exam this weekend. – What will you have this weekend?

The manager teaches us how to do our jobs. – Who teaches us how to do our jobs?

●設定

関係：アルバイト先の先輩と後輩

目的：面接を受け採用される

●会話例（空所に適文を選んで記号を入れなさい）07

In the waiting room at the store, a clerk has an interview with you:

CLERK: (Looking at your resume) Are you a freshman at the university?

YOU: Yes. I would like to work at this store.

CLERK: Are you enjoying school?

YOU: (1)

CLERK: When did you move here?

YOU: I moved here a month ago.

CLERK: (2)

YOU: Yes, I only have classes in the morning.

CLERK: Really? Are you free in the afternoon?

YOU: Yes, but I can't work this weekend.

CLERK: What will you do this weekend?

YOU: I must study for my midterm exam this weekend.

CLERK: Okay, you don't have to do the job this weekend. (3)

YOU: Does that mean I got the job?

CLERK: Yes, you'll learn how to do the job.

YOU: Who teaches us how to do our jobs?

CLERK: The manager teaches us how to do our jobs.

YOU: (4)

CLERK: No, I just started working here last week.

㋐ Can't you teach them?

㋑ I'm a quick learner.

㋒ Do you have much time to work?

㋓ Can you work on any other days?

Ⓐキーワードやキーセンテンスを指摘しましょう。

Ⓑ補充された会話を聴いた上で、上記の会話例をペアで音読してみましょう。

Create a dialogue

今までの作業を踏まえ、ペアになってオリジナルの会話を作成しましょう（提出は別紙を使用してもいい）。

Ⓐこの Unit の最初のページを参考に「アルバイトについて話す」英文を 3 つ作成しましょう。

① ______________________________.

② ______________________________.

③ ______________________________.

Ⓑこの Unit の 2 ページ目を参考に「アルバイトについて聴く」英文を 3 つ作成しましょう。

① ______________________________.

② ______________________________.

③ ______________________________.

Ⓒ上記の英文を使って 6 行ほどの会話原稿を作成し音読してみましょう。

Ⓓ第三者に聞いてもらい、感想を自己評価の参考にしましょう（各項 2 点満点、他の項目を加えてもいい）。

①発音、アクセント　（　　　　点）

②語順、文法　（　　　　点）

③切り方　（　　　　点）

④強弱　（　　　　点）

⑤目線　（　　　　点）　（合計　　　　/10 点）

Ⓔ仕事について話すときに使われる語句をリストアップしましょう（オリジナル作成時に用いた語句も追加）。

① you don’t have to come：来なくていい

②

③

④

⑤

Unit 7

疑問詞の文 …………………………… 旅行について

●写真の人物の立場で想像し、例を参考に英語で書きなさい。

Ⓐ自己

① We met this spring.

② We have the same class.

③ One of our classmates has a car.

④ ______________________________.

⑤ ______________________________.

Ⓑ予定

⑥ We are going to visit the amusement park.

⑦ We are planning to stay at the youth hostel for two nights.

⑧ More than six people can fit in this car.

⑨ ______________________________.

⑩ ______________________________.

Ⓒ希望

⑪ Our leader wants to arrive at the destination tonight.

⑫ One member of our group hopes to eat local dishes.

⑬ My brother wants to go with us.

⑭ ______________________________.

⑮ ______________________________.

Grammar（疑問詞の作り方）

●下線部を問う疑問詞の文（空所を補充しましょう）

Ⓐ We're planning to stay ❶<u>at the youth hostel</u> ❷<u>for two nights</u>.

→❶を問う　Where are we going to stay for two nights?

→❷を問う　__________ __________ are we planning to stay at the youth hostel?

Ⓑ ❶<u>Our leader</u> wants to arrive ❷<u>at the destination</u> ❸<u>this night</u>.

→❷を問う　Where does our leader want to go tonight?

→❸を問う　______________ does our leader want to arrive at the destination?

→❶を問う　______________ wants to arrive at the destination tonight?

●質問／応答

Ⓐ Your brother/sister and you are at home

① You: I'm in a hurry. Cram school starts at 6 o'clock.

Your sister: How __________ you go there?

You: I'll go __________ bicycle. I'm late!

② You: __________ you use my bicycle yesterday?

Your sister: I didn't use it. __________ is the matter?

You: I can't find the key.

Ⓑ The manager and you are at the convenience store

① Manager: Someone asked me what time you would finish your job today.

You: Who __________ you that?　＊疑問詞が主語の場合「疑問詞＋動詞」

Manager: One of the customers asked me.

② You: May I take a break?

Manager: How ______________ ______________ you be gone?

You: I'll be gone for about thirty minutes. Please look after the store.

Dialogue

●描写と質問　前ページの英文を踏まえ、描写と質問の英文セットを作成。

① We are going to visit the amusement park. – Where are we going?

② More than six people can fit in this car. – How many people can fit in this car?

③ My brother wants to go with us. – Who wants to go with us?

●設定

関係：大学の友人同士

目的：行先や車での旅行について話す

●会話例（下の質問に答えなさい）08

You are in the back seat of the car with your friend. Her boyfriend will drive:

You: Is he accustomed to driving?

Your friend: Yes. (　　1　　) He owns this car.

You: I see. Where are we going?

Your friend: We're going to visit the national park.

You: (　　2　　)

Your friend: No. But he must take rests during the trip.

You: That's good. We have to be safe.

Your friend: His car is comfortable and roomy, too.

You: How many people can fit in this car?

Your friend: I think more than six people can fit.

You: (　　3　　)

Your friend: Does anyone else want to go with us?

You: Yes.

Your friend: Who wants to go with us?

You: My brother might come. He likes to travel by car.

Your friend: Really? We can ask your brother to take us on a drive!

You: Uh, he doesn't have a driver's license.

Your friend: (　　4　　)

You: I wish one of us had a driver's license.

ア He goes to university by car.

イ We still need another driver.

ウ We can invite more people to go on the trip with us.

エ Aren't you going to drive?

Ⓐキーワードやキーセンテンスを指摘しましょう。

Ⓑ補充された会話を聴いた上で、上記の会話例をペアで音読してみましょう。

Create a dialogue

今までの作業を踏まえ、ペアになってオリジナルの会話を作成しましょう（提出は別紙を使用してもいい）。

Ⓐこの Unit の最初のページを参考に「旅行について話す」英文を 3 つ作成しましょう。

① .

② .

③ .

Ⓑこの Unit の 2 ページ目を参考に「旅行について聴く」英文を 3 つ作成しましょう。

① .

② .

③ .

Ⓒ上記の英文を使って 6 行ほどの会話原稿を作成し音読してみましょう。

Ⓓ第三者に聞いてもらい、感想を自己評価の参考にしましょう（各項 2 点満点、他の項目を加えてもいい）。

①発音、アクセント（　　点）

②語順、文法（　　点）

③切り方（　　点）

④強弱（　　点）

⑤目線（　　点）　（合計　　/10 点）

Ⓔ仕事について話すときに使われる語句をリストアップしましょう（オリジナル作成時に用いた語句も追加）。

① be accustomed to 〜 ing：〜することに慣れている

②

③

④

⑤

Unit 8

完了形と仮定法 ………………… 人を紹介する

●写真の人物の立場で想像し、例を参考に英語で書きなさい。

Ⓐ状況

① She may be able to find our meeting place.

② The train has arrived on time.

③ She has visited this city before.

④ ______________________________________.

⑤ ______________________________________.

Ⓑ人物

⑥ She likes traveling.

⑦ She has traveled many places.

⑧ We have been friends for many years.

⑨ ______________________________________.

⑩ ______________________________________.

Ⓒ願望

⑪ She wants to visit many places.

⑫ It's a weekday today.

⑬ The train arrived at 11:45.

⑭ ______________________________________.

⑮ ______________________________________.

Grammar（完了形と仮定法）

●完了形　have（has）＋過去分詞

have（has）＋動詞（過去分詞形）で「〜してきた」「〜したことがある」「〜してし まった（〜したところ）」という表現ができます。現在までの時間の推移を意識した「現在完了形」と呼ばれる形です。

（　　）内の動詞を適切な形にものに直し記入しましょう。

① She ______ here since 2010. (live)
② My father ______ dinner already. (cook)
③ The teacher ______ me yesterday. (help)
④ How long ______ you ______? (sleep)

⑤ They ______ the mountain three times. (climb)
⑥ We have never ______ to Europe. (be)
⑦ Some actors ______ parts in this drama two years ago. (play)
⑧ How many times ______ she ______ this novel? (read)

⑨ The train ______ already ______. (leave)
⑩ He ______ not ______ his assignment yet. (finish)
⑪ Who ______ just ______ to the station? (come)

●仮定法　助動詞（過去）＋動詞

助動詞の過去形や完了形を使って、事実に反する仮定を表すことができます。和訳をしなさい。

① I wish I could ask my sister.（現在における仮定）

______.

② He might have joined our club if he attended this university.（現在における仮定）

______.

③ I should have studied English in school.（過去における仮定）

______.

④ We could have succeeded in business with his advice.（過去における仮定）

______.

＊ if+SV 〜 や with(without) ＋が加わることで、条件が示される場合もあります。

Dialogue

●描写と質問 前ページの英文を踏まえ、描写と質問の英文セットを作成。

① She has traveled many places. – Has she traveled many places?

② We have been friends for many years. – Have you been friends for many years?

③ The train arrived at 11:45. – What time did the train arrive?

●設定

関係：人を迎えに行く友人と自分

目的：人を紹介する

●会話例（空所に適文を選んで記号を入れなさい） 09

In the morning, on the way to the station:

FRIEND: My friend is about to arrive at the station.

YOU: Have you been friends for many years?

FRIEND: Yes. Her name is Ayako. We have been friends since high school.

YOU: (1)

FRIEND: She still lives in my hometown.

YOU: Really? (2)

FRIEND: She wants to visit many places.

YOU: Has she traveled many places?

FRIEND: Yes, she is a seasoned traveler. We've arrived at the station.

YOU: Can you find her?

FRIEND: (3) It's a weekday today. There are so many people here.

YOU: What time did the train arrive?

FRIEND: At 11:45.

YOU: (4)

FRIEND: At the North Exit.

YOU: You'd better call her.

FRIEND: (on the phone) We're here. Where are you now? Are you at the North Exit?

YOU: Oh! We're at the South Exit! We should have met at the ticket gate.

㋐ I'm looking for her.

㋑ Where does she live now?

㋒ Which part of the station are we going to meet?

㋓ It must take a long time to get here.

Ⓐキーワードやキーセンテンスを指摘しましょう。

Ⓑ補充された会話を聴いた上で、上記の会話例をペアで音読してみましょう。

Create a dialogue

今までの作業を踏まえ、ペアになってオリジナルの会話を作成しましょう（提出は別紙を使用してもいい）。

Ⓐこの Unit の最初のページを参考に「人を紹介する」英文を 3 つ作成しましょう。

① ______________________________.

② ______________________________.

③ ______________________________.

Ⓑこの Unit の 2 ページ目を参考に「知らない人について尋ねる」英文を 3 つ作成しましょう。

① ______________________________.

② ______________________________.

③ ______________________________.

Ⓒ上記の英文を使って 6 行ほどの会話原稿を作成し音読してみましょう。

Ⓓ第三者に聞いてもらい、感想を自己評価の参考にしましょう（各項 2 点満点、他の項目を加えてもいい）。

①発音、アクセント　（　　　　点）

②語順、文法　（　　　　点）

③切り方　（　　　　点）

④強弱　（　　　　点）

⑤目線　（　　　　点）　（合計　　　　/10 点）

Ⓔ仕事について話すときに使われる語句をリストアップしましょう（オリジナル作成時に用いた語句も追加）。

① Let me introduce ～：～を紹介させて

②

③

④

⑤

Unit 9

進行形と受動態……場所を案内する

●写真の人物の立場で想像し、例を参考に英語で書きなさい。

Ⓐ案内

① I'm going to Professor Allen's class.

② The office is near the entrance.

③ They are walking by a row of trees.

④ ______________________________.

⑤ ______________________________.

Ⓑ特徴

⑥ Room 205 is located in the South Hall.

⑦ They were built about 80 years ago.

⑧ The staff is preparing for the school festival.

⑨ ______________________________.

⑩ ______________________________.

Ⓒ成果

⑪ The professors are helping us to get jobs.

⑫ They are praising each other for passing the exam.

⑬ Many overseas students are admitted to this university.

⑭ ______________________________.

⑮ ______________________________.

Grammar（進行形と受動態）

進行形　be+ 〜 ing

状態の be 動詞、動作の一般動詞、両者は同一の文に共存しませんが、「進行中の動作」は状態的側面もあり、be+ 〜 ing の形を取ります。

空所を補充してそれぞれ進行形の文（〜しているところだ）にしましょう。

① I will write a letter. → I ______ ______ a letter

② He checks the result. → He ______ ______ the result

③ They listen to his speech. → They ______ ______ to his speech.

④ The crowd rushed into the station. → The crowd ______ ______ into the station.

受動態　be+ 〜 ed（過去分詞）

「〜られる」という受け身の表現も be 動詞と一般動詞を組みまわせて作ります。空所を補充しましょう。

① TV ______ ______ by them.（観られる）

② The dinner ______ ______ by my father.（料理される）

③ The package ______ ______ by the policeman.（発見された、過去）

④ They ______ ______ by the teacher.（褒められた、過去）

進行形・受動態の否定・疑問

① I ______ ______ ______ a letter.（書いていない）

② ______ he ______ the result?（調べていますか？）

③ TV ______ ______ ______ by them.（観られない）

④ ______ the dinner ______ by my father?（作られましたか？）

●描写と質問 前ページの英文を踏まえ、描写と質問の英文セットを作成。

① I'm going to Professor Allen's class. – Whose class are you going to?

② Room 205 is located in the South Hall. – Is it located in the South Hall?

③ They were built about 80 years ago. – When were they built?

●設定

関係：場所を知る人と知らない人

目的：場所を案内する

●会話例（空所に適文を選んで記号を入れなさい） 道案内　歴史　認知度　就職率　ゼミ　10

On campus, before class:

YOU: Whose class are you going to?

STUDENT: I'm going to Professor Allen's class.

YOU: Me, too. (　　1　　)

STUDENT: It's in room 205.

YOU: Is it located in the South Hall?

STUDENT: Yes, it's located in the South Hall.

YOU: Thank you. By the way, these buildings look very old. When were they built?

STUDENT: They were built about 80 years ago.

YOU: They look like ancient buildings.

STUDENT: Our university has a long history. (　　2　　)

YOU: Some of the professors are well-known, too.

STUDENT: Yes, there are many popular seminars.

YOU: Will the professors help us to get jobs?

STUDENT: Of course.

YOU: I see, (　　3　　)

STUDENT: The seminar rooms are located in the East Hall.

YOU: You know this university so well. (　　4　　)

STUDENT: This is my second freshman year. I failed some classes last year.

㋐ So, many people know about it.

㋑ Where is it held?

㋒ You must not be a freshman!

㋓ Where are the seminar rooms?

Ⓐキーワードやキーセンテンスを指摘しましょう。

Ⓑ補充された会話を聴いた上で、上記の会話例をペアで音読してみましょう。

Create a dialogue

今までの作業を踏まえ、ペアになってオリジナルの会話を作成しましょう（提出は別紙を使用してもいい）。

Ⓐこの Unit の最初のページを参考に「場所を案内する」英文を 3 つ作成しましょう。

① ____.

② ____.

③ ____.

Ⓑこの Unit の 2 ページ目を参考に「場所を聴く」英文を 3 つ作成しましょう。

① ____.

② ____.

③ ____.

Ⓒ上記の英文を使って 6 行ほどの会話原稿を作成し音読してみましょう。

Ⓓ第三者に聞いてもらい、感想を自己評価の参考にしましょう（各項 2 点満点、他の項目を加えてもいい）。

①発音、アクセント（　　点）

②語順、文法（　　点）

③切り方（　　点）

④強弱（　　点）

⑤目線（　　点）　（合計　　/10 点）

Ⓔ仕事について話すときに使われる語句をリストアップしましょう（オリジナル作成時に用いた語句も追加）。

① go straight down：まっすぐ進む

② turn right (left)：右に（左に）曲がる

③ around the crossing：交差点の周りに

④ you can see (find)：見えるでしょう

⑤ how can I get to：どう行けばいいですか

⑥

⑦

⑧

⑨

⑩

Unit 10

分詞・動名詞・不定詞 ……… 予定をすり合わせる

●写真の人物の立場で想像し、例を参考に英語で書きなさい。

Ⓐ予定

① I have plans to shop that day.

② A hike is scheduled next week.

③ I am going to see a convenience store manager who's hiring a new staff.

④ ______________________________.

⑤ ______________________________.

Ⓑ実績

⑥ It is hard to support myself.

⑦ I have finished arranging the products on the shelves.

⑧ This is my university diploma.

⑨ ______________________________.

⑩ ______________________________.

Ⓒ夢

⑪ My dream is to be a translator.

⑫ Graduating from a foreign university is one of my dreams.

⑬ I enjoy touring hot springs around Japan.

⑭ ______________________________.

⑮ ______________________________.

Grammar（分詞・動名詞・不定詞）

●分詞

～ ing には、名詞を修飾する働きもあります（1 語なら前から、2 語以上なら後ろから）。形を変えなさい。

① The ________ boy is my cousin. (wait)

② The boy ________ by the gate is my cousin. (wait)

～ ed などの過去分詞も名詞を修飾します。

③ He has a ________ machine. (repair)

④ He has a machine ________ by the staff. (repair)

●動名詞

～ ing はそれ自体で名詞「～すること」の意味になります。形を変えなさい。

① ________ a speech is a requirement. (make)

② She enjoyed ________ her speech. (make)

＊不定詞（to 動詞）も名詞「～すること」の意味になります。形を変えなさい。

③ ________ other people's speeches is useful. (hear)

④ It's useful ________ other people's speeches. (hear) ＊ it = to ～

⑤ She wants ________ other speeches. (hear) ＊願望の動詞は to 動詞を従える

⑥ My mother told me ________ the dishes. (wash) ＊ tell, want も「人」と to 動詞を従える

●不定詞

to 動詞には、形容詞「～するための」や副詞「～するために」の働きもあります。空所を自由に補いましょう。

① We have plans to visit ________.

② It is time to ________. ＊「時」を表す場合 it を主語に

③ I go to university to ________.

Dialogue

●描写と質問　前ページの英文を踏まえ、描写と質問の英文セットを作成。

① I have plans to shop on that day. – Do you have any plans on that day?

② It is hard to support myself. – Is it hard to support yourself?

③ My dream is to be a translator. – What is your dream?

●設定

関係：店長とアルバイト

目的：予定をすり合わせる

●会話例（空所に適文を選んで記号を入れなさい）　仕事内容　入る日時　互いの目的　夢　11

At the backdoor of the convenience store, after work:

MANAGER: Can you work next Sunday? Do you have any plans that day?

YOU; Well, I have plans to shop on that day. I have to get my PC repaired.

MANAGER: I see. (　　1　　)

YOU: I'll be able to come.

MANAGER: Will you?

YOU: I can buy a better computer now.

MANAGER: I see, then you'll come next Sunday?

YOU: Yes. I'll be here. (　　2　　)

MANAGER: Is it hard for you to support yourself?

YOU: Yes, but supporting myself is important.

MANAGER: I'm working hard to realize my dreams, too.

YOU: What is your dream? My dream is to be a translator.

MANAGER: My dream is to be a professional bowler.

YOU: Really? (　　3　　) Are you good at bowling?

MANAGER: Well, I have to go bowling every day to become a professional.

YOU: (　　4　　)

MANAGER: Yes. We're going to be short-handed, that's why I want you to work Sunday.

㋐ I must work to pay university expenses.

㋑ I'll ask someone else, then.

㋒ Are you planning to go bowling next Sunday?

㋓ That's news to me!

Ⓐキーワードやキーセンテンスを指摘しましょう。

Ⓑ補充された会話を聴いた上で、上記の会話例をペアで音読してみましょう。

Create a dialogue

今までの作業を踏まえ、ペアになってオリジナルの会話を作成しましょう（提出は別紙を使用してもいい）。

Ⓐこの Unit の最初のページを参考に「予定を述べる」英文を 3 つ作成しましょう。

① ______________________________.

② ______________________________.

③ ______________________________.

Ⓑこの Unit の 2 ページ目を参考に「予定を聴く」英文を 3 つ作成しましょう。

① ______________________________.

② ______________________________.

③ ______________________________.

Ⓒ上記の英文を使って 6 行ほどの会話原稿を作成し音読してみましょう。

Ⓓ第三者に聞いてもらい、感想を自己評価の参考にしましょう（各項 2 点満点、他の項目を加えてもいい）。

①発音、アクセント　（　　　点）

②語順、文法　（　　　点）

③切り方　（　　　点）

④強弱　（　　　点）

⑤目線　（　　　点）　（合計　　　/10 点）

Ⓔ予定をすり合わせるときに使われる語句をリストアップしましょう（オリジナル作成時に用いた語句も追加）。

① When are you free?：いつ時間がありますか？

② Which date is convenient?：何日が都合いいですか？

③ confirm (reconfirm)：確認する（再確認する）

④ have trouble coordinating：調整するのに困っている

⑤ match your schedule：あなたにスケジュールを合わせる

⑥

⑦

⑧

⑨

⑩

Unit 11

接続詞と関係詞……………イベントの詳細を知る

●写真の人物の立場で想像し、例を参考に英語で書きなさい。

Ⓐ趣向

① I like playing the guitar.

② We are playing folk rock.

③ This guitar was given to me by my friend's brother.

④ ______________________________.

⑤ ______________________________.

Ⓑイベント詳細

⑥ A music festival is held every year.

⑦ We are scheduled to play on Sunday afternoon.

⑧ If it rains, the festival will be postponed.

⑨ ______________________________.

⑩ ______________________________.

Ⓒ気分

⑪ Playing music gives me energy.

⑫ I am a little nervous because this is my first time.

⑬ I am moved by the song which I will sing solo.

⑭ ______________________________.

⑮ ______________________________.

Grammar（接続詞と関係詞）

●接続詞

二つの SV をつなぐのが接続詞です。接続詞に導かれる前半を理解し、後半（主文）を自由に補いなさい。

① When I return home, I'll ________________________.

② Because I don't have money, I ________________________.

③ Though I was happy at the party, I ________________________.

④ If it rains tomorrow, I ________________________.

⑤ If I were you, I ________________________.

＊ I think (know, believe) that he's honest.

＊ I wonder why (whether, when, where) she will come.

That や疑問詞も接続詞として機能します。

●関係詞

直前の名詞（先行詞）を SV のまとまりで修飾するときつなぎになるのが関係詞です。

先行詞と共通する部分が who, which, whose などに変わって修飾側の SV が続きます。空所を埋めましょう。

Ⓐ I know the boy + He speaks English./My mother met him./His father is a doctor.

→① I know the boy ____________ speaks English.

② I know the boy ____________ my mother met.

③ I know the boy ____________ father is a doctor

Ⓑ She has a bag + It was made in Italy./I presented it to her last year./Its color is deep blue.

→① She has a bag ____________ was made in Italy.

② She has a bag ____________ I presented to her last year.

③ She has a bag ____________ color is deep blue.

Ⓒ My classmate will participate in the athletic event, which excites me.（文全体を修飾）

Ⓓ when, where, why, how も先行詞を修飾する SV を導きます。

① This is the castle. + They went there last March.

→ This is the castle ________ they went last March.

= This is the castle to which they went last March.

② Her advice is the reason ________ I tried to take the entrance exam.

③ Using the internet is ________ I search for word definitions.

Dialogue

●描写と質問 前ページの英文を踏まえ、描写と質問の英文セットを作成。

① We are playing folk rock. – What kind of music are you playing?

② We are scheduled to play on Sunday afternoon. – When are you scheduled to play?

③ I am a little nervous. – How do you feel now?

●設定

関係：学園祭の出演者（音楽、バンド）と友人

目標：イベントの詳細を知る

●会話例（空所に適文を選んで記号を入れなさい） 12

PERFORMER: I'm going to play on stage with the band at the campus festival.

YOU: Great! What kind of music are you playing?

PERFORMER: We're playing folk rock, which is very popular.

YOU: When are you scheduled to play?

PERFORMER: Sunday afternoon.

YOU: (1) How do you feel now?

PERFORMER: I'm a little nervous because this is the first time for me to play on stage.

YOU: I think you must be a good performer.

PERFORMER: I recommend that you sit up front.

YOU: It's crowded, it'll be difficult to sit up front.

PERFORMER: (2)

YOU: It'll be wonderful. Lots of people will attend!

PERFORMER: (3)

YOU: You play on an outdoor stage, so if it rains we may get wet.

PERFORMER: If it rains, it will be held on Monday.

YOU: Monday? I can't come because I'm going to perform that day.

PERFORMER: You are? (4)

YOU: Let's hope it doesn't rain.

㋐ The weather report says that it's going to rain that day.

㋑ I didn't know you were a musician.

㋒ You'd better come early.

㋓ That's tomorrow!

Ⓐキーワードやキーセンテンスを指摘しましょう。

Ⓑ補充された会話を聴いた上で、上記の会話例をペアで音読してみましょう。

Create a dialogue

今までの作業を踏まえ、ペアになってオリジナルの会話を作成しましょう（提出は別紙を使用してもいい）。

Ⓐこの Unit の最初のページを参考に「イベントを説明する」英文を 3 つ作成しましょう。

① ________________.

② ________________.

③ ________________.

Ⓑこの Unit の 2 ページ目を参考に「イベントについて聴く」英文を 3 つ作成しましょう。

① ________________.

② ________________.

③ ________________.

Ⓒ上記の英文を使って 6 行ほどの会話原稿を作成し音読してみましょう。

Ⓓ第三者に聞いてもらい、感想を自己評価の参考にしましょう（各項 2 点満点、他の項目を加えてもいい）。

①発音、アクセント　（　　　　点）

②語順、文法　（　　　　点）

③切り方　（　　　　点）

④強弱　（　　　　点）

⑤目線　（　　　　点）　　（合計　　　/10 点）

Ⓔイベントの詳細を話すときに使われる語句をリストアップしましょう（オリジナル作成時に用いた語句も追加）。

① open on time：時間通りに始まる

② call the staff：スタッフを呼ぶ

③ Is this seat available?：この座席は空いてますか？

④ buy a ticket at the door：当日券を買う

⑤ box office：切符売場

⑥

⑦

⑧

⑨

⑩

Unit 12

第4・第5文型 …………………………… 不安を取り除く

●写真の人物の立場で想像し、例を参考に英語で書きなさい。

Ⓐ不安

① I am worried that I may have failed the interview.

② I left one of the application questions blank.

③ Many students find it difficult to be self-assertive.

④ ____.

⑤ ____.

Ⓑ準備

⑥ I asked the company to send me a brochure.

⑦ I have a recommendation written by my professor.

⑧ The TOEIC test revealed my weak points.

⑨ ____.

⑩ ____.

Ⓒ自己分析

⑪ I have a serious personality.

⑫ My experience working part-time was useful.

⑬ Diligence is my strongpoint.

⑭ ____.

⑮ ____.

Grammar（第 4・第 5 文型）

●第 4 文型（SVOO）

SV 後に O（目的語）が二つ「〜に〜を」ある文を第 4 文型といいます。空所を自由に補いましょう。

① I gave her a guidebook.

② She gives me ______________________.

③ They sent their mayor ______________________.

④ He showed me the way to ______________________.

⑤ The teacher told the students that they should ______________________.

●第 5 文型（SVOC）

SV 後に O（目的語）と、それを補う C（補語）がくるのが第 5 文型です。

I saw her sing.（I saw + she sigs）

I saw him running.（I saw + he is running）

We heard the information announced.（OC の関係が受動的 we heard + the information was announced）

My mother made me wash her car.　＊ make, have, let は使役表現「〜させる」です。

＊ OC を従える動詞として、他に call（〜を〜と呼ぶ）. leave, keep（〜を〜のままにする）など

O と C の関係に気をつけながら、空所を自由に補いましょう。

① The students see the teacher ______________________.

② Many visitors felt the paintings ______________________.

③ We found the classmate ______________________.

④ The captain made the members ______________________.

⑤ People call the player ______________________.

⑥ The staff left the window ______________________.

⑦ You should keep the room ______________________.

⑧ We elected that candidate ______________________.

Dialogue

●描写と質問 前ページの英文を踏まえ、描写と質問の英文セットを作成。

①I am worried that I may have failed the interview. – What are you worried about?

②Taking the TOEIC test revealed my weak points. – What did the TOEIC test revealed?

③Diligence is my strong point. – What is your strong point?

●設定

関係：就職準備に悩む友人

目的：不安を取り除く

●会話例（空所に適文を選んで記号を入れなさい）内容　詳細　出番　気分　13

YOU: You're wearing a suit today! Are you going somewhere special?

FRIEND: The interview training is today but ...

YOU: What are you worried about?

FRIEND: I am worried that I may have failed in the interview.

YOU: That was just practice. Take it easy.

FRIEND: Have you taken the TOEIC test? It helped me improve my English.

YOU: What did the TOEIC test reveal?

FRIEND: It revealed my weak points. (　1　)

YOU: Did the interviewer ask you for your TOEIC score?

FRIEND: I'm sure I'm going to be asked for my TOEIC score.

YOU: (　2　) What is your strongpoint?

FRIEND: I don't know. I'm struggling with that question.

YOU: (　3　)

FRIEND: I'm thinking about that every day!

YOU: That may be your strongpoint.

FRIEND: What? The fact that I don't know my strongpoints?

YOU: You're thinking about it every day, so that means, you're diligent. It's a positive fact!

FRIEND: Diligence is my strongpoint. That's true! (　4　)

㋐I don't have good enough skills to communicate in English.

㋑Thank you, I will tell the interviewer!

㋒You'd better tell the interviewer about your strongpoints.

㋓However, you don't know what they are.

Ⓐキーワードやキーセンテンスを指摘しましょう。

Ⓑ補充された会話を聴いた上で、上記の会話例をペアで音読してみましょう。

Create a dialogue

今までの作業を踏まえ、ペアになってオリジナルの会話を作成しましょう（提出は別紙を使用してもいい）。

Ⓐこの Unit の最初のページを参考に「不安を訴える」英文を 3 つ作成しましょう。

① ＿＿＿＿＿＿＿＿＿＿＿＿＿＿＿＿＿＿＿＿＿＿.

② ＿＿＿＿＿＿＿＿＿＿＿＿＿＿＿＿＿＿＿＿＿＿.

③ ＿＿＿＿＿＿＿＿＿＿＿＿＿＿＿＿＿＿＿＿＿＿.

Ⓑこの Unit の 2 ページ目を参考に「不安を聴く」英文を 3 つ作成しましょう。

① ＿＿＿＿＿＿＿＿＿＿＿＿＿＿＿＿＿＿＿＿＿＿.

② ＿＿＿＿＿＿＿＿＿＿＿＿＿＿＿＿＿＿＿＿＿＿.

③ ＿＿＿＿＿＿＿＿＿＿＿＿＿＿＿＿＿＿＿＿＿＿.

Ⓒ上記の英文を使って 6 行ほどの会話原稿を作成し音読してみましょう。

Ⓓ第三者に聞いてもらい、感想を自己評価の参考にしましょう（各項 2 点満点、他の項目を加えてもいい）。

①発音、アクセント　（　　　　点）

②語順、文法　（　　　　点）

③切り方　（　　　　点）

④強弱　（　　　　点）

⑤目線　（　　　　点）　（合計　　　　/10 点）

Ⓔ不安を取り除くときに使われる語句をリストアップしましょう（オリジナル作成時に用いた語句も追加）。

① cheer up：励ます

② effort is rewarded：努力は報われる

③ as you think：あなたが思うように

④ go for it：頑張ろう

⑤ don’t work too hard：頑張りすぎないで

⑥

⑦

⑧

⑨

⑩

Note

Motivator **Composition and Dialogue** [B-905]
会話と表現のクラスワーク

1　刷　2020年 3月 26日

著　者　高橋　哲郎　Tetsuro Takahasi

発行者　南雲　一範　Kazunori Nagumo
発行所　株式会社　南雲堂
〒162-0801　東京都新宿区山吹町361
NAN'UN-DO Co., Ltd.
361 Yamabuki-cho, Shinjuku-ku, Tokyo 162-0801, Japan
振替口座 : 00160-0-46863
TEL: 03-3268-2311（営業部：学校関係）
03-3268-2384（営業部：書店関係）
03-3268-2387（編集部）
FAX: 03-3269-2486

編集者　加藤　敦

本文デザイン　奥定　泰之

装　丁　Nスタジオ

検　印　省　略

コード　ISBN978-4-523-17905-4　C0082

Printed in Japan

E-mail　nanundo@post.email.ne.jp
URL　http://www.nanun-do.co.jp/